Sch

H www.heinemann.co.uk/library

Visit our website to find out more information about **Heinemann Library** books.

To order:
☎ Phone 44 (0) 1865 888066
🖹 Send a fax to 44 (0) 1865 314091
💻 Visit the Heinemann Bookshop at www.heinemann.co.uk/library to browse our catalogue and order online.

Heinemann Library
Halley Court, Jordan Hill, Oxford, OX2 8EJ
a division of Reed Educational and Professional Publishing Ltd

OXFORD MELBOURNE AUCKLAND
JOHANNESBURG BLANTYRE GABORONE
IBADAN PORTSMOUTH (NH) USA CHICAGO

Heinemann is a registered trademark of Reed Educational and Professional Publishing Ltd

Text © Anne Geldart, 2002

First published in 2002

ISBN 0 431 14974 7 (hardback)
06 05 04 03 02
10 9 8 7 6 5 4 3 2 1

ISBN 0 431 14981 X (paperback)
07 06 05 04 03
10 9 8 7 6 5 4 3 2 1

British Library Cataloguing in Publication Data
A catalogue record for this book is available from the British Library

Typeset by Artistix, Thame, Oxon
Printed and bound in Spain by Edelvive

Acknowledgements
The publishers would like to thank the London Beth Din, Kashrut Division, for permission to use the kosher certificate, p. 19.

The publishers would like to thank the following for permission to use photographs: Andes Press Agency/Carlos Reyes-Manzo, pp. 14, 16 (bottom right), 23 (top), 24 (top), 43; BFI Stills, p. 2 (left); The Bridgeman Art Library/Galleria degli Uffizi, Florence, p. 5; The Bridgeman Art Library/Magyar Nemzeti Galeria, Budapest, p. 58; The Bridgeman Art Library/The Mass Gallery, London, p. 12; The Bridgeman Art Library/Museum of the City of New York, p. 49; Camera Press/Titti Fabi, p. 3 (right); Camera Press/Amram Galmi/Imapress, p .13; Camera Press/Lee Lynx, p. 6; Camera Press/Greg Marinovich, p. 28; Camera Press/Richard Stonehouse, pp. 3 (left), 8; Camera Press/Kevin Unger, p. 48; Corbis, p. 56; Mary Evans Picture Library, p. 55; Impact/John Evans, p. 52; Alex Keene, p. 17; Performing Arts Library/Mark Douet, p. 2 (right); Zev Radovan, pp. 10, 15 (left), 16 (bottom left and top right), 20, 21, 23 (bottom), 24 (bottom), 37, 38, 42; Science Photo Library/Gordan Garradd, p. 50; Science Photo Library/Royal Observatory, Edinburgh, p. 59; Science Photo Library/TEX Image, p. 53, Science Photo Library/Hattie Young, p. 40; Juliette Soester, pp. 15 (right), 18, 25, 33, 34, 45, 46.

The publishers have made every effort to contact copyright holders. However, if any material has been incorrectly acknowledged, the publishers would be pleased to correct this at the earliest opportunity.

Websites
Links to appropriate websites are given throughout the book. Although these were up-to-date at the time of writing, it is essential for teachers to preview these sites before using them with pupils. This will ensure that the web address (URL) is still accurate and the content is suitable for your needs.

We suggest that you bookmark useful sites and consider enabling pupils to access them through the school intranet. We are bringing this to your attention as we are aware of legitimate sites being appropriated illegally by people wanting to distribute unsuitable and offensive material. We strongly advise you to purchase suitable screening software so that pupils are protected from unsuitable sites and their material.

If you do find that the links given no longer work, or the content is unsuitable, please let us know. Details of changes will be posted on our website.

The Bible
Jews call the Bible Tenakh. It is mainly written in Hebrew, but some parts are in Aramaic, a language similar to Hebrew. The Tenakh has three parts: Torah (the Five Books of Moses), Nevi'im (the books of the Prophets) and Ketuvim (holy writings). In this book, whenever we say 'the Bible' it is the Tenakh that we refer to. For English-speaking pupils, the quotations are taken from English translations and can be found in the school Bible.

Tel: 01865 888058 www.heinemann.co.uk

Contents

Introduction to Judaism

In this section you will:

- learn why it is important to study religions so that we can know about what people believe and how this affects the way they live
- read about the Hebrew language and where it is used.

What is Judaism?

Judaism is the name of the religion that Jewish people follow. It began with Abraham in about 2000 BCE. Judaism started in the land now called Israel, but from 70 CE, most Jews have lived in other countries.

Christians and Muslims share many of the beliefs of the Jews. They use stories and teachings of the **Tenakh** (the Hebrew Bible).

The Tenakh is like a library of books, arranged in three sections. These are the **Torah** (first five books), the **Nevi'im** (prophets) and **Ketuvim** (holy writings). You will learn more about the Tenakh later in this book.

Judaism is a **monotheistic** religion. That is, Jews believe in only one God. This God is the creator of all things, and judges all people.

Many Jews believe God chose them to be his people. He made a **covenant** (promise) with them. They must follow the laws that God revealed to Moses. The Ten Commandments are the most important of these laws, and Christians and Muslims, as well as Jews, think they are important today.

Joseph on the West End Stage

Moses' story in The Prince of Egypt

2

Vanessa Feltz, a famous Jewish television presenter

Woody Allen, a famous Jewish film-maker

Jews also believe that Israel (the country) is important to their history, as well as in the present day.

Stories of importance

Many films and musicals are based on stories from the Tenakh. These stories are also shown in pictures in art galleries.

In today's world, there are many famous Jews. Jonas Salk developed the polio vaccine. Michael Marks (of Marks & Spencer) and entertainers Barbara Streisand and Woody Allen are also Jewish.

The writers and thinkers Sigmund Freud and Karl Marx were from Jewish families.

The book *The Diary of Anne Frank* is about the suffering of the Jews in World War II.

Hebrew – as easy as A B G – yes, 'G'!

Most Jews learn to read the Hebrew language as part of their religious studies. This is because most of the Tenakh, the Jewish Bible, is written in Hebrew.

Hebrew is one of the oldest written languages. The first three letters are Alef, Bet and Gimel. The Hebrew 'Alefbet' has 22 letters, which are all consonants. Sometimes Hebrew vowel sounds are shown by making small marks above, below or alongside the consonants. The Tenakh is marked in this way.

Newspapers in Israel do not show the vowels at all. This means readers must fill in these sounds for themselves.

Abraham

An easy life?

It would be nice to have an easy life, with money, servants and not having to work – being able to relax.

There was a man called Abram, who was very rich. He lived about 4000 years ago in the city of Haran in modern-day Iraq. He was married to Sarai. Abram believed God told him to leave his home and go and search for a new land. He was quite old, and had to start a new life with his wife, and their nephew, Lot.

Living the easy life

Abram becomes Abraham

You can read about this in Genesis, the first book of the **Tenakh**.

In those days, a name was important because it said something about the person's character. Abram meant 'exalted father'. When Abram proved himself to be obedient to God, he was re-named Abraham, which means 'Father of nations'. His wife's name, Sarai, was also changed to Sarah, which means 'princess'.

These name changes marked the beginning of a special relationship between God and the descendants of Abraham. Jews believe this was the **covenant**, an agreement in which God says 'I will be your God and you shall be my people'.

The sign of the covenant was **circumcision**. This is where the foreskin of a boy's or man's penis is removed by a surgical operation. Jews continue this tradition today.

Destruction of Sodom and Gomorrah

Abraham, Sarah and Lot, their nephew, travelled towards the new land that God had promised them. Lot decided to leave and go to live in the city of Sodom and a neighbouring city of Gomorrah.

The ancient story tells that the people in these cities were very wicked and God decided to destroy them. Abraham prayed to God to ask if some good people could be saved. Lot was saved. His wife was told not to look back at the city. She did look back – and was turned to a pillar of salt.

Sacrifice

Abraham and Sarah wondered when they would have the son that God had promised them. Then, when they were quite old, Sarah became pregnant. They named their son Isaac.

When Isaac was twelve years old, Abraham believed that God wanted him to offer his son as a sacrifice. He took him to a high mountain, and was just about to offer him as a sacrifice when he heard a voice telling him to stop. The voice told him to kill a ram that God had provided instead.

This was a sign that God does not want human sacrifice. He wants people to be obedient to Him.

Abraham, about to sacrifice Isaac

Father Abraham

Abraham is important to Muslims and Christians, as well as to Jews.

Jewish people believe that Abraham is the father of their nation through his son, Isaac. Muslims believe that Abraham is the founding father of their faith through his other son, Ishmael. They see him as one of the first Muslim **prophets**, or messengers of God.

Christians believe that Abraham's faith, rather than his actions, was the most important thing. It was his faith that made God look on him with favour. Because of Abraham's great faith, God promised Abraham that he would have as many descendants as there were grains of sand on the seashore.

There are now millions of Jews, Muslims and Christians all over the world who look to Abraham as a role model of someone who is faithful and obedient to God.

Moses

In this section you will:
- think about what makes a good leader
- learn about the importance of Moses as a leader who obeyed God
- read about the story of Moses and the golden calf.

What makes a leader?

A leader is someone who other people choose to follow. Leaders may have a strong personality and a clear idea of where they want to lead people. Modern politicians are examples of leaders.

Moses the leader

Several hundred years after Abraham, the Jews had become slaves of the Egyptians. Moses was a Jew, but he was adopted by the Egyptian royal family when he was a baby. One day, he saw a Jewish slave being beaten by a slave master.

David Ben-Gurion, a modern Moses

This made him angry and he killed the slave master. He ran away, and eventually met and married Zipporah, the daughter of a man who owned many thousands of sheep. Moses became a shepherd.

One day he thought he saw a bush that was burning but was not being burnt up. He believed that God was telling him to return to Egypt and put things right for the Jews.

At first Moses did not want to go. He felt he was not the right man for the job. But then he became convinced that God had called him to set the Jewish people free, and that he must obey.

> Some people believe that Moses saw a bush that really was on fire and heard the voice of God. Others believe Moses had a 'vision' – a mind-picture – of the bush on fire.

The Passover

Moses went to Pharaoh, the king of Egypt, and told him that God said, 'Let my people go'. Pharaoh refused. Then ten plagues happened. A plague is a disease or terrible event. Moses said that God sent the plagues. This helped the Jews to believe that God had chosen Moses to be their leader. Moses told them that God was on their side and was trying to help them.

Still Pharaoh refused to let the Jews go. Then in a final plague, the Angel of Death visited each house and killed the oldest child. The Angel of Death passed over the homes of the Jews. They had smeared lamb's blood on their door-posts to show

Many Jews today see Moses as an important role model. He is seen as a good leader, and one who was obedient to God. He is also the one who taught the Jews about the Law and about justice.

The ten plagues sent to Egypt

they were Jews. This is now called **Pesach**, which means 'Passover'. Pharaoh finally let the Jews go and they escaped from Egypt. This escape is called the **Exodus**.

The lawgiver

Moses led the Jewish people to Mount Sinai. There, tradition says, he met God face to face and received God's teachings, the **Torah**, which includes the Ten Commandments.

Finally, after forty years, Moses led the people to the border of the land that he said God had promised them. However, he died before they entered the Promised Land.

The golden calf

The Torah tells the story of Moses and the golden calf. It is a reminder to Jews to worship the one true God.

Moses went up to Mount Sinai to receive the Ten Commandments from God. He left his brother, Aaron, in charge of the Israelites. Whilst Moses was away, the Israelites asked Aaron to make a golden calf. In Egypt, people used to worship the golden calf, which was a symbol of strength. The Israelites wanted to worship it, too. Aaron agreed, and a golden calf was made.

When Moses returned, he was really mad! He threw the stone tablets with the Ten Commandments on them and smashed them on the ground. His people had broken the law of God which said that they should not worship an idol. He made them destroy the golden calf.

Aaron and the people were very sorry. Aaron later became chief priest to the community. His descendants served as priests in the temple in Jerusalem for hundreds of years.

Elijah

Good anger

Sometimes it is right to get angry. In 1985, Bob Geldof, a rock musician, was very angry because people were starving in Africa. He thought people were not doing enough to help. He organized a charity concert called Live Aid. This raised over £40 million.

Bob Geldof's anger helped millions through Live Aid

Elijah gets angry

Jews believe that all through history, God sent prophets to tell people His message. They tell people what God says is wrong with the world, and call them to be more obedient to God. In this way, they can help to bring about a better world. One of the most important of these prophets is Elijah. You can read about him in your Bible, in 1 Kings: 17–19.

He lived in about the ninth century BCE when King Ahab and Queen Jezebel ruled Israel. Elijah thought the King and Queen were leading the people to worship false gods.

Showdown at Mount Carmel

Queen Jezebel came from Sidon, where the people worshipped Baal. She wanted the Jews to worship Baal, too, and had over 450 prophets to encourage them to do so.

Elijah became angry and believed God wanted him to take on these prophets of a false god.

He challenged them to a contest on Mount Carmel, the 450 prophets of Baal on one side, and Elijah alone on the other. They each prayed to their god to set fire to their sacrifices. It was Elijah's prayer that succeeded, and his sacrifice that was consumed by fire. This was a sign that God was the true and only God.

Earthquake, wind and fire

A still, small voice

After this, Queen Jezebel wanted to kill Elijah, so he went into hiding. He was scared, depressed and alone. He hid in a cave, and prayed for God to appear to him.

There was an earthquake, but God did not appear. Then there was a fire, but God still did not appear. Then Elijah heard a still, small voice and this was God, speaking to him. This shows that God can be known in small events, as well as in exciting, spectacular events.

Naboth's Vineyard

If anyone inherited land in Israel, they were not allowed to sell it to the King. This was the law. King Ahab noticed his neighbour, Naboth, had a vineyard next to the palace. He wanted to buy it, but Naboth refused.

Ahab was upset, so his wife, Queen Jezebel hired two men to lie about Naboth. They said he was rude about the king and about God. He could be put to death for this.

When Elijah heard about it, he confronted Ahab. Ahab asked for God's forgiveness.

The end of the story

Tradition says Elijah never died but was taken directly to heaven in a chariot. Many Jews today believe that Elijah will return when the **Messiah** (God's representative) is coming to the earth. At the annual celebration of **Pesach**, an empty chair is set at the table. This is called Elijah's chair.

What is a prophet?

A prophet is someone who speaks for God – a kind of messenger. God chooses prophets to give messages or teachings to the people. Prophets were role models to the Israelites, and they had to be especially holy.

The Hebrew word for prophet is 'navi'. This comes from 'navi sefatayim', which means 'fruit of the lips'. The prophet's words were the 'fruit of the lips'. The prophets gave their messages to the Israelites when they felt inspired by God.

Many Jews believe that Moses was the greatest prophet of all. Prophets who came after him, they say, repeated many of the original teachings that Moses passed on from God. The teachings and stories of the Jewish prophets are found in the Bible. The prophets' words are read out in **synagogues** today.

Beliefs 1 – God and the covenant

In this section you will:
- learn why belief in one God is important to Jews
- understand why the **covenant** is important.

Promises, promises

We often feel hurt or disappointed when people don't keep their promises to us. We depend on promises. For example, marriage involves promises between two people to love and care for and be faithful to each other.

Jews believe that God has promised to care for them and has chosen them to be His people. In return they must be faithful and obedient to Him. This is called the covenant.

Jews believe God made the first covenant with Noah after the flood (Genesis 9) and gave the rainbow as a sign that He would never destroy the whole world again.

The second covenant was with Abraham, when God promised him many descendants (Genesis 12 and 17). This was renewed with Moses when God gave him the Ten Commandments and other teachings that the people had to follow.

'I am the Lord your God, who brought you out of the land of Egypt, out of the house of slavery. You shall have no other gods besides me.'

Exodus 20: 2–3

When Jewish families have their sons circumcised (see pages 40–1), or their children become **Bar Mitzvah** or **Bat Mitzvah** (see pages 42–3), they are confirming the covenant.

Marriage involves making promises

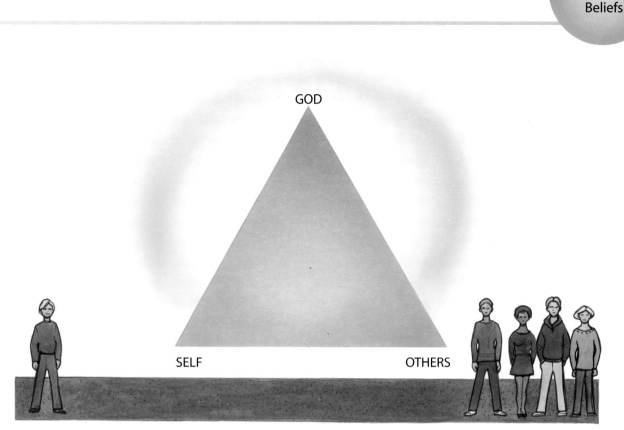

Martin Buber's triangle of relationships

Monotheism

'Hear, O Israel! The Lord is our God, the Lord is one. You shall love the Lord your God with all your heart, and with all your soul and with all your might.'

Deuteronomy 6: 4

This quotation is called the **Shema**. 'Shema' is Hebrew for 'hear'. The Shema is written on a small scroll of parchment called a **mezuzah** (see pages 14–15) and put in a small case that is fixed to the doorposts of many Jewish homes.

The idea of having one God is called **monotheism**. Jews were one of the first groups to believe in one God who creates everything, and keeps everything going. He is Judge and King of the Universe. Jew believe they must not worship **idols**.

The Jewish thinker, Martin Buber, wrote a book called *I and Thou*. He said people

needed a relationship with God and this would help them to have proper relationships with each other.

Jeremiah on the covenant

The **Tenakh** mentions the covenant 300 times. The prophet Jeremiah reminded the Israelites that they needed to keep the covenant with God. He said that the temple in Jerusalem would be destroyed, and that God would make a new covenant with them afterwards. He wrote:

'This is the covenant that I will make with the house of Israel after that time, says the Lord. I will put my law in their minds and write it on their hearts. I will be their God and they will be my people.'

Jeremiah 31: 33

Beliefs 2 – shalom

In this section you will:
- learn about the Jewish idea of **shalom**
- read about ways in which Jews put shalom into practice.

Give me some peace!

There does not seem to be much peace in our world. People fall out

- at school
- at home with their relatives
- anywhere they get together.

We read about wars in the newspapers and wonder if there has ever been any peace in the world.

The dove of peace

So, what is peace?

Jews often use the word 'shalom' in place of 'hello' or 'goodbye'. It is the Hebrew word for 'peace'.

Some Jewish teachers say that peace begins inside you. If you are in a bad temper, you have no peace inside you, so you cannot help someone else to find peace. A Jewish writer, Louis Jacobs, says, 'Peace is the fruit of inner strength.'

It is important to have peace within the family. Parents and children must all try to live in a peaceful way.

Jewish people believe that sometimes it is right for people to fight in wars. However, they long for a time when wars will cease.

There are many different groups within **Judaism**. They have differing thoughts about their religion. Many believe an age of peace will come when God sends his Anointed One, Mashiah (**Messiah**).

The **prophet** Isaiah describes the age of peace like this:

The wolf shall live with the lamb.
The leopard with the kid.
The calf and the young lion will be together
and a little child shall lead them.
The cow and the bear shall graze,
their young shall lie down together;
the lion shall eat straw like the ox.
The nursing child shall play
over the hole of the asp,
and the weaned child shall put its hand on the adder's den.

They will not hurt or destroy on all my
holy mountain:
for the earth will be full of the knowledge
of the Lord
as the waters cover the sea.

Isaiah 11: 6 (contemporary English version)

Peace is about bringing opposite sides
together, so that they understand each
other. This is what Isaiah was saying in his
word-picture of nature coming together.

Let the sun rise to light the morning,
Even the purest prayer will not awaken
Bitter tears will not revive, will not bring
back
Those whose candle was put out and
buried in the dust.
Don't say a day will come, seize that day
for it is not a dream
And in all the squares
Shout out a song for peace!

The Song of Peace

Israel's Prime Minister, Yitzak Rabin, was
assassinated in 1995 while he was trying
to bring peace to the country of Israel. He
was carrying in his jacket pocket a poem
written by two Jewish men called *The
Song of Peace*.

*Yitzak Rabin, Prime Minister of Israel, was
assassinated for his beliefs*

Shalom in action

Jews come together at the Shalom
Centre in Philadelphia, USA. They
study and work in the fields of
politics and social issues, such as the
care of the earth and the need to
bring peace in the Middle East. They
also have meetings with members of
other religions. They encourage
people to pray and to reflect on the
needs of the world.

They believe that the **Torah** teaches
about social justice and the need to
care for nature. This is because the
Creator God made the world. They
also believe there should be a
balance between work and rest. This
is important so that people can
spend time thinking about the way
they live.

13

Signs and symbols 1

In this section you will:
- learn about symbols that are important to Jewish people
- understand how symbols can say more than words.

What is a symbol?

A symbol is something that stands for something or someone else. A sign is a picture or gesture that is used instead of words.

Symbols are often used in religion. They may convey ideas that are too difficult to put into words.

Magen David Adom

No one knows for sure when the Star of David (**Magen David Adom**) became a symbol in the Jewish faith. It may have been an ancient Hindu symbol.

The Magen David Adom

An image of this star was found in a **synagogue** in Capernaum from the first century CE.

When Adolf Hitler came to power in Germany in the 1930s, he ordered Jews to wear the Star of David. This made it easier for the Nazis to identify them. By the end of World War II, the Nazis had murdered six million Jews.

After the War, when the country of Israel was set up, the new country included the Star of David in its national flag.

The menorah

In many religions, light is an important symbol for good. The **menorah** was part of the official 'furniture' of the ancient temple. Today most **synagogues** have a menorah. It is a six-branched candleholder.

A special, eight-branched candleholder called a **hanukiah** is used at the celebration of **Hanukkah**, in the winter.

The mezuzah

'These commandments which I have given you this day are to be remembered and taken to heart; repeat them to your children…Bind them as a sign upon your hand and wear them as a pendant on your forehead; write them on the door posts of your houses and on your gates.'

Deuteronomy 6: 6–9
(Contemporary English Version)

This girl is lighting the hanukiah

A mezuzah is often found on every door of a Jewish home

If you visit a Jewish home today, you may see small containers like the one above.

This is a **mezuzah** case and is fixed to the door frame of every room in the house except the bathroom. It contains a small scroll on which is written the **Shema**.

Even actions or gestures can be symbols. For example, folding the hands and bowing the head when praying are symbols of humility. The action of lighting a candle is symbolic of the first action of God in creation when He said, 'Let there be light'.

'To life!'

The Chai symbol, which means 'life', is often used on jewellery that Jewish people wear.

Jewish people may say, 'L'chayim', which means 'To life!', when they raise their glasses in a toast. Chai also stands for the number 18. When Jewish people give gifts to charity, they often give them in sets of 18, for this reason.

Signs and symbols 2

In this section you will:
- learn about several of things that matter to Jews
- think about what matters to you.

The tefillin

What matters to you most?

If your house caught fire, what would you save first? It might be a toy or a computer or a photograph that means a lot to you. Some things will be more important to you than others.

Tallit

Many Jewish people wear a **tallit** when they pray. This is a prayer robe or shawl. A full-size tallit is about 2 metres by 1.5 metres.

Tefillin

Tefillin are small leather boxes which contain tiny scrolls. The **Shema** prayer is written on the scrolls. They wear them on their head and their arm as a sign that they are true to God.

The tallit

The kippah

Men visit the mikveh before **Yom Kippur**, an important Jewish festival. Men and women visit the mikveh before the marriage ceremony. Women visit the mikveh after their monthly period has ended or after childbirth.

The idea behind this is that the person must be clean inside as well as outside. By dipping themselves under the water of the mikveh, Jewish people believe they have become purified and so fit to talk to God in prayer.

The mikveh is used for ritual bathing

Kippah

A **kippah** is a cap that some Jews wear all day, while others wear a kippah only for prayer. The kippah may be plain, or decorated with symbols such as the **Magen David Adom**. It is a sign of humility to God.

The mikveh

The **mikveh** is a special pool where people can immerse themselves to be purified. This is not about physical cleanliness. A Jew would have to be clean outside even before going into the mikveh.

The Hamesh hand

Many Jewish people wear a design called the Hamesh hand as part of a necklace or a bracelet. There may be an eye in the centre of the hand, with Hebrew writing around it.

The Hamesh hand represents the hand of God. It is God who will protect all his people. No one knows why it is a popular symbol for Jewish people. A hand is also a popular symbol in many eastern religions, where it is believed to protect against evil.

Kosher food

In this section you will:
- learn about the importance of **kosher** food to Jewish people
- read about different types of kosher food.

You are what you eat

Food is important to everyone. A vegetarian does not eat meat products. A vegan will avoid anything that comes from animals, such as milk or cheese. What people eat or refuse to eat shows what they believe.

Kosher food

The word kosher means clean, pure and fit to eat. Many Jews try to follow the laws about what they can and cannot eat from the **Torah**.

The book of Leviticus, the third book of the Torah, gives rules about food that is fit to eat. When the book of Leviticus was written, the ancestors of the Jews lived in the deserts. The food rules were for their good health. Now Jews obey them as an act of obedience to God.

As a general rule, animals that have cloven (divided) hooves and chew the cud are fit to eat. This means cows, sheep and goats are kosher. Pigs, rabbits and horses are not kosher.

Fish are kosher if they have fins and scales, like trout and cod. Shell-fish and prawns are not kosher.

Birds such as chicken, duck and turkey are allowed, but birds of prey are not kosher.

Eggs and milk are kosher if they come from kosher birds and animals.

There are many different types of kosher food

Vegetables and fruit are neutral. They are allowed, as long as they are clean and are carefully checked for bugs and 'creepy-crawlies'.

Strict Jews also try to obey the rule that says they must not eat meat and milk foods at the same meal. In an **Orthodox** (very strict) Jewish home, there are often two sinks, sets of crockery and cutlery for milk and meat foods.

For strict Jews, it is important that kosher food is properly labelled. Some supermarkets have special kosher sections. Kosher food usually has a special label on it to show that a **rabbi** has approved it.

Some years ago there was a rumour that Coca-Cola was made in a non-kosher way. The company was so concerned that they invited a leading rabbi to visit one of the plants where Coca-Cola is made. He approved it – Coca-Cola was declared to be kosher.

Sometimes, Jewish people set up their own shops and have their own butchers.

In London's East End, a group of Jews set up a Kosher Luncheon Club. They specialized in fish dishes. It became popular with lots of people who lived in the area, not just Jews.

A kosher food certificate

Popular kosher dishes

Jewish people have created many different kosher dishes over the years. Here are some popular kosher dishes.

Knishes are dumplings made from potatoes and flour. They are often stuffed with a savoury mixture of minced liver, onions and potato. *Knish* is Ukrainian for 'dumpling'.

Bagels are doughnut-shaped pieces of bread. They may have sesame seeds sprinkled on top. Bagels are very popular in the USA.

Matzah ball soup is often served at the festival of **Pesach** (Passover), but may be eaten at other times, too. Matzah balls are made from matzah meal, which is crumbs of a bread made without yeast.

You can find out more about Jewish cooking at this website: http://www.jewfaq.org/food.htm.

Worship at home 1 – Shabbat

In this section you will:
- think about the need for rest and time to think
- learn about the importance of the day of **Shabbat** to Jews.

Holy days and holidays

Everyone needs to take some time off from work. Originally, days of rest and relaxation were linked with holy days. Now any time off is called a holiday.

Weekends are an important time to rest for most people. For Jews, weekends are special.

Jews measure a day from sunset to sunset. From sunset on Friday to sunset on Saturday is a day of rest for Jews and it is called by the Hebrew word Shabbat (Sabbath). Some Jews measure Shabbat from a set time on Friday (say 6pm) to the same time on Saturday.

Why is there Shabbat?

'On the seventh day, having finished all his work, God blessed the day and made it holy, because it was the day when he finished all his work of creation.'

Genesis 2: 2–3

'Remember to keep the Sabbath day holy. You have six days to labour and do all your work, but the seventh day is the Sabbath of the Lord your God; that day you must not do any work, …for the Lord made the heavens and the earth in six days, the sea and all that is in them, and on the seventh day he rested. Therefore the Lord blessed the Sabbath day and called it holy.'

Exodus 20: 8–9

These verses from the **Torah** explain why Jews observe Shabbat. It is a weekly day of rest to remember and be thankful to God for His work of creation.

Shabbat today

Before Shabbat begins, the family must clean the house and get it ready. All the shopping must be done before Friday evening. The table will be set with the 'best' tablecloth, cutlery and plates.

Some Jewish men and women go to the **synagogue** on Friday evening, while others will go on Saturday morning.

Just before Shabbat, the mother of the family lights two candles and says a special prayer to welcome in this day of rest. She says a blessing for her family and the candles are a symbol of joy and peace.

The father blesses his chidren and says the **kiddush** (blessing) over a cup of wine. The family sits down to a meal together.

On the table are two plaited loaves called **challot** (singular **challah**). These remind Jews of the double-helping of **manna** (special bread) that God provided in the desert when they had escaped from Egypt. This was so they would not have to work on Shabbat.

No work must be done on Shabbat, and Jews try to avoid anything that encourages work. For some Jews, this means that even turning on a light must be avoided, although some have automatic timers for ovens and lights.

Havdalah is a ceremony that marks the end of Shabbat. The word means 'separation'. There is a spice box that is passed round as a symbol of hope for good things to come during the week ahead, and a plaited candle to remind Jews that God's first act in creation was to make light. There are more blessings:

● over a last cup of wine

● over the spices to show that the spiritual part of the week has gone and the 'ordinary' day is about to begin

● over the candle-flame to show that Jews may once again light a fire, and finally, a blessing to thank God for providing a holy day of rest.

A spice box

Preparing for Shabbat

Shabbat is a very special occasion for Jewish people. Some of the ways Jews get ready for Shabbat are:

● phone round the family to wish them a happy Shabbat

● start preparing food for Shabbat at the beginning of the week

● have best clothes ready to wear on Shabbat

● only do what *must* be done before the start of Shabbat

● do not let Shabbat preparations cause trouble or rows among the family.

Worship at home 2 – prayer

In this section you will:
- learn about the importance of worship at home to Jewish people
- read about ways in which Jewish people pray.

Worship begins at home

Jews believe that it is good for a family to pray together. It helps them to think about each other's needs.

At many festivals, including **Shabbat**, Jews may worship at home and at the **synagogue**.

In **Orthodox** synagogues women do not pray aloud. But many women lead the prayers at home.

Why pray?

The family is very important to Jews. They believe that the **covenant** between God and the Jews means they should try to get closer to God. They can do this through prayer.

They may also pray if they need to ask for something for themselves or someone in need. However, Jews believe they must only pray for good reasons. They must not pray for evil or selfish reasons.

Reading the Siddur

Jews also pray to thank God for the good things He has done for them. They worship God because they believe He created the world, and it was He who rescued the people of Israel from slavery in Egypt.

Types of prayer

Most Jews use a prayer book called a **Siddur**. This contains prayers they can use at home or the synagogue. These are printed in Hebrew, but some have English translations alongside.

Prayers begin with the **Shema** (see page 16). This is followed by the **amidah** – eighteen benedictions, or blessings. Each one ends with:

'Blessed art Thou, O Lord our God, King of the Universe.'

Many of the prayers come from the Bible, such as this one:

'Holy, holy, holy, is the Lord of Hosts, The whole earth is full of your glory.'

Most of the time Jews pray standing, but may bow as they refer to God as King. At certain high holy days, such as **Yom Kippur** (see pages 32–3) Orthodox Jews may kneel as a sign of humility before God. For prayer, Jewish men and some women wear the prayer robe or **tallit**, and a **kippah** and **tefillin** (see page 16).

Ready for prayer

How to pray

There are many special prayers in **Judaism**, and special times when Jews pray. But prayers can also be said at any time, as this story shows.

A young Jew was finding it difficult to pray. He asked a rabbi for help. The rabbi replied: '… Go into a field to pray. Even the grasses will join you. They will give you strength. When no words come – do not worry. Just wanting to speak to God is a great thing. Even if all you say to God is "Help!" it is still good. Repeat this over and over again until God opens your lips and words begin to flow from your heart.'

Worship in the synagogue

In this section you will:
- learn why the **synagogue** is important to Jewish people
- read about what happens there and about the work of the **rabbi**.

The Torah scrolls are taken from the Ark

Places that matter

We all have special places, places that matter to us. It may be the place we were born, or where we go on holiday.

For Jewish people, the places where they meet to worship God have always been special. For about a thousand years, until the first century CE, they worshipped in a temple in Jerusalem and in local places of worship. When the temple was destroyed, they worshipped in synagogues.

The synagogue

The word synagogue means a place of meeting. The Hebrew for this is **Bet ha Knesset**. The synagogue may also be called the House of Study or the House of Prayer.

What do you see inside a synagogue?

Every synagogue has a cupboard called **Aron Hakodesh** (the Ark). This is where the scrolls of the **Torah** and other holy writings are kept. The scrolls may be 'dressed' in a mantle of expensive cloth.

The shield represents the breastplate worn by priests in the ancient temple. There is a pointer called a **yad** which is used to point to the words on the scrolls when reading during services. The bells look like crowns and remind worshippers that the Torah is the teaching of the great King – God.

Sometimes families pay for new scrolls in memory of an important event in their lives.

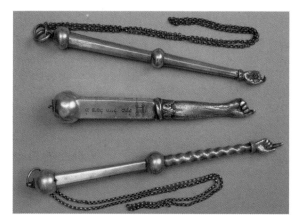

Yad pointers come in a variety of styles

Inside a synagogue

Above Aron Hakodesh is **Ner Tamid**, the perpetual light. This is a sign of God's **covenant**. Also above the Ark are two tablets, which represent the Ten Commandments given to Moses.

In the centre of the synagogue is the **bimah**, a raised platform. On this is a reading desk, where the scrolls rest while readings of the **sidra** (portions of scripture) take place.

An important person at synagogue services is the **rabbi**, who is leader of the synagogue. His main role is to teach and explain the Torah. Another is the **cantor**, who leads the singing in the services. There are also **wardens**, who help people to find their seats.

There are differences between **Orthodox** and **Reform** synagogues, which we will look at in the next section.

Important events take place at the synagogue, such as **Bar Mitzvah**, **Bat Mitzvah** and weddings. Sometimes families pay an annual sum for the upkeep of the synagogue and to pay the salary of the rabbi and other staff at the synagogue.

The work of a rabbi

The word 'rabbi' means 'teacher' or 'master'. A rabbi is a highly respected member of the Jewish community. In Orthodox synagogues, rabbis are always men. In non-Orthodox synagogues, women can be rabbis.

Rabbis study for many years before they can lead a congregation. They must have a good knowledge of the Torah, the **Talmud** and the **Mishnah**.

Rabbis give a talk at the main service in the synagogue. They may explain the meaning of the readings from the Torah. They also organize a religious school for Jewish children. They lead services such as weddings and funerals, and Bar and Bat Mitzvot. Rabbis often give advice to Jews, both in the synagogue and in the community.

Orthodox and Reform synagogues

In this section you will:
- learn about **Orthodox** and **Reform synagogues**
- read about the Bevis Marks synagogue in London.

Tradition or change?

Not so long ago a computer would fill a whole room. Now we can fit one into a watch. Television and the Internet help us to see what is happening all over the world. Women have more rights than they did in years gone by.

Is all change good? Is it sometimes better to let things stay as they are?

Religious people have to face this problem, too. They have to decide whether to keep their religion as it was when it first began, or bring it up-to-date.

Jewish groups

Secular Jews are not religious, but feel they belong to their Jewish roots. **Ashkenazim** are Jews whose ancestors came from Eastern Europe. **Sephardim** are Jews who can trace their families back to Spain and North Africa.

Two of the largest Jewish groups are Orthodox Jews and Reform Jews.

Orthodox Jews believe they should keep to the old ways. They believe it is right to observe the traditions and festivals as set out in the **Torah**. They believe these teachings are still relevant today.

They look forward to the coming of the **Messiah**, who will bring a time of peace.

Reform Jews believe you can adapt the old teachings to present-day situations. For example, they believe that the **kosher** food laws were right when Jews lived in the desert. They think it is not necessary to keep these laws now because we have modern methods of storing and cooking food. They believe that every Jew should work to bring peace into the world. It is not right to wait for a Messiah figure to bring a golden age.

In Orthodox synagogues, men and women sit separately. In Reform synagogues, men, women and children all sit together.

Orthodox synagogues always have a male rabbi, while in the Reform synagogue there may be a male or female **rabbi**.

Orthodox families start their **Shabbat** at sunset on Friday, which varies throughout the year. Reform families tend to start at 6pm on Fridays.

Inside an Orthodox synagogue

A woman rabbi reading the Torah in a Reform synagogue

In an Orthodox synagogue in Britain, the Shabbat service is in Hebrew, except for the prayers for the royal family and the State of Israel. In Reform synagogues, more of the service is in English.

In Orthodox synagogues there are only males in the choir and no musical instruments are used. Reform synagogues may have a mixed choir and an organ to accompany the singing.

The **minyan** – a minimum of ten people for public worship to take place – in an Orthodox synagogue must be men. In Reform synagogues the minyan may contain women.

All synagogues have prayer services throughout the week. They also have schools where young people can learn about the faith and the history of the Jewish people.

The Bevis Marks synagogue

A famous synagogue in Britain is the Bevis Marks synagogue in London. A number of Jewish refugees from Spain and Portugal settled in London in the mid-1600s CE. They built the present Bevis Marks synagogue in 1701 CE. It has remained almost unchanged since that time. It has a large candelabrum, which was a present from a Dutch synagogue in Amsterdam.

Today, the synagogue holds many services, sometimes in Portuguese in memory of the original members.

The Written Torah

In this section you will:
- think about how books influence your own lives
- learn about some of the important writings that Jews refer to for help in their lives and worship.

The power of books

Ray Bradbury wrote a book called *Fahrenheit 451*. This was a fictional story about a time when a government burned books because it was afraid of the power they had to make people think for themselves.

Reading the Torah at the Western Wall

Scriptures

Scripture is the name given to the writings of religions. They are important to people because they are about the events, people and teachings that are central to their beliefs.

Jews believe their holy writings, especially the **Torah**, teach the way God would like them to live.

The Torah

'Blessed art Thou, O Lord God of the Universe, who hast chosen us from all people and hast given us thy Torah.'

This is the blessing said before the reading from the Torah in the **synagogue**.

Torah is the name given to the five books of Genesis, Exodus, Leviticus, Numbers and Deuteronomy.

The Torah contains stories of creation, the early leaders of the Jews and the story of Moses and the escape from Egypt. The Torah also contains the 613 **mitzvot** (rules) that were given to Moses. The Ten Commandments are included in the 613 mitzvot.

There are 248 positive and 365 negative mitzvot. The prayer robe often has 613 strands to remind Jews of these rules.

It is hard to remember so many rules. Some rules are not clear. Over the years, **rabbis** and teachers have discussed the meanings. One teacher was Rabbi Hillel in the first century CE. He wrote:

'What is hateful to you, do not do to your neighbour. That is the whole of the Torah. All else is commentary.'

Many Jewish children attend **cheder**, a school for the study of Torah. Some may go on to enter **Yeshiva**, a college for more advanced study.

Orthodox Jews believe that the Torah is the word of God and cannot be changed. Other Jews believe that it is all right to interpret the writings to fit in with modern life. For example, non-Orthodox Jews may not observe the **kosher** food laws or they may allow a woman to become a **rabbi**.

Nevi'im and Ketuvim

Jews use the word 'Torah' to mean:

- the first five books of the Bible
- the whole of the **Tenakh** (the Written Torah)
- the later teachings that explain the Tenakh (the Oral Torah)

The other two parts of the Tenakh are called **Nevi'im** and **Ketuvim**.

The Nevi'im contain the historical books about the Kings of Israel and the writings of the prophets such as Isaiah.

The Ketuvim are books of poetry, songs and wise sayings, and includes the Psalms, Proverbs and the story of Job.

Words from the Torah

'Do not desire another person's property: not their house; their partner, their slaves, their cattle, their donkeys – or anything else.'
Exodus 20: 17

'I am the Lord your God and I command you – do not make fun of the deaf or cause a blind person to stumble.'
Leviticus 19: 14

'When you lend money to people, you are allowed to keep something of theirs to ensure they pay back the loan. But do not take their millstones that they use to grind grain to make into flour, or else they may starve.'
Deuteronomy 24: 6

The Oral Torah

In this section you will:

● learn about the importance of the Mishnah, the Talmud and other Jewish writings

● read and reflect upon some of the wise sayings from the Talmud.

How is law made?

Law is always changing. Parliament makes laws, and courts have to uphold these laws.

However, sometimes courts have to apply laws to particular cases. The court may have to take into account aspects that the lawmakers did not consider.

Jewish scriptures have developed in similar ways.

First came the **mitzvot** in the **Tenakh**. Then, if the teachings of the Tenakh are too hard to understand, Jews have other writings that explain the Tenakh. As well as the Written **Torah** (the Tenakh) they can turn to the Oral Torah. This is a collection of the ideas of scholars and rabbis that try to make these laws clear.

A law court in action

The Mishnah

The word **Mishnah** is Hebrew for 'to repeat, to study'. The Mishnah is the written version of the Oral Torah. It was written down in about 200 CE. It deals with things such as when to plant seeds, and how to prepare for and observe **Shabbat** and other festivals. It has sections about marriage, divorce, buying and selling, legal matters, sacrifices and the rules about purity.

Rabbi Judah the Prince collected and carefully edited these sayings.

The Talmud

The **Talmud** took over 800 years to complete. It includes ideas of over 2000 Jewish teachers and rabbis. There are stories to help people to understand how to live, called **agadah**, which means 'telling'. There are halakhot (singular **halakhah**). These are teachings about how ancient laws can apply to new problems.

The Talmud contains some wise sayings such as:

● the health of the body depends upon the teeth

● charity knows no race or creed

● breakfast is the most important meal of the day.

The Midrash

Midrashim are writings based on stories from the Tenakh, and the agadah. The writers often used examples from real life to explain the difficult parts of the Tenakh.

How are these holy writings used today?

Jewish people refer to the Talmud, the Mishnah and the Midrash to help them to understand the meaning of the Written Torah. They do this to help them to put these teachings into practice. Judges in the Rabbinical courts (called **Bet Din**) may use them in divorce or inheritance cases.

Wise sayings from the Talmud

Here is a collection of wise sayings from the Torah. They contain important rules and ideas for the Jewish community.

● No one may eat until the animals have been fed.

● If someone says you have the ears of a donkey, take no notice. If two people tell you – get yourself a saddle!

● When clouds are bright, they contain little water.

● Ambition destroys those who have it.

● A person should try to be flexible like a reed, but as hard as cedar wood.

● A parent should treat all their children alike.

Festivals 1 – Yom Kippur

In this section you will:
- learn about the importance of **Yom Kippur** to Jewish people
- read about Yom Kippur and the scapegoat
- learn about the Days of Repentance.

Times to celebrate, times to think

Festivals help religious people to think about important aspects of their faith. Festivals can also help us to find answers to some important questions people ask. These questions are about how people ought to behave and what matters most in life.

I can't forgive myself…

Have you ever done something that made you feel really guilty? Perhaps you did or said something cruel or nasty. Did you find it hard to forgive yourself?

We all need to forgive ourselves sometimes

Jews believe that justice and forgiveness go together.

At Yom Kippur, Jews ask God and other human beings to forgive them.

What is Yom Kippur?

Yom Kippur means 'the Day of **Atonement**'. Atonement means to put right what you have done wrong in a practical way. On Yom Kippur, Jews also try to put things right with God. To do this, they know they have to ask God to forgive them, and to promise to change what is wrong with their lives.

Rosh Hashanah is Jewish New Year, and it falls in September or October. At this time, Jews remember God as creator. For ten days after New Year, the 'Days of Return', they make an effort to put things right that they have done wrong. Then on Yom Kippur, they remember God as Judge.

For a month before Yom Kippur, Jews hear the **shofar**, a ram's horn, as it is blown in the **synagogue**. This reminds them they need to ask for forgiveness. They also need to **repent**, that is, to turn away from their wrong ways, and turn back to God.

'On the tenth day of the seventh month, you must fast.'

Leviticus 16: 29

To **fast** is to give up food for a religious reason.

The day before Yom Kippur, Jews prepare themselves. They may use the **mikveh**, a special bath used to purify themselves.

They then eat their last meal before beginning a twenty-five hour fast.

'To know what it is to be hungry, even for a single day, encourages pity for the hungry, the oppressed and the unfortunate.'

Louis Jacobs, Jewish thinker

On Yom Kippur, Jews avoid sexual intercourse. They do not wear leather shoes. People used to think wearing leather shoes was showing off their wealth.

They spend the day in prayer, and try to settle any arguments they have with other people.

At the end of Yom Kippur, there is a service in the synagogue. They see the doors of the **Aron Hakodesh** (Ark) open wide. This is a way of saying that God wants to accept them. They hear the shofar once more, to signal the end of the day.

Blowing the shofar

The Days of Repentance

The Days of Repentance is the period of ten days before the festival of Yom Kippur. It is a time to prepare for the festival. Jews try to put right anything which is wrong in their lives, perhaps by saying sorry to people for things they have done to hurt them.

Yom Kippur and the scapegoat

In the days of the temple in Jerusalem, Jewish priests used to sacrifice animals on Yom Kippur. They used to read out the sins of the people over the head of a goat. They then led the goat out of the city and pushed it over a cliff to its death. This was a sign that the people's sins were dealt with.

Festivals 2 – Purim

In this section you will:
- learn why the festival of **Purim** is important to Jews
- read about the custom of Haman's pockets.

The festival story

You can find the story of Purim in the book of Esther.

Many years ago, the Persian army invaded Israel. They took some Jews to their capital city, Susa. Two of the captives were Esther and her cousin, Mordecai.

One day, the King of Persia, Xerxes, ordered his wife, Queen Vashti, to come to a party. She refused. The King was angry. His advisers told him he should divorce her before anyone heard about what she had done.

The King's prime minister, Haman, set out to find a new queen.

Jewish children performing a Purim play

Among the girls taken to the King's palace was Esther. Mordecai told Esther she must not let the king know that she was a Jew.

King Xerxes thought Esther was the most beautiful of all the girls, and he married her.

Haman hated the Jews, especially Mordecai, and planned to kill them. He drew lots (like a lottery) to see what day he would murder Mordecai and the rest of the Jews.

Mordecai heard about Haman's plot. He asked Esther to talk to the King while in his private room. Women were not allowed to approach the king, on pain of death. Esther was not afraid. She told the King she was Jewish, and about Haman's plot.

The King was angry with Haman. That night, at dinner, he told Haman he knew Esther was Jewish and that he knew about his plan. He ordered his guard to hang Haman on the gallows he had built for Mordecai. The Jews were saved.

After this, Haman's friends were punished, and the Jews were allowed to defend themselves against attack.

Purim today

Purim is the name for 'lots' and this gave the festival its name.

The festival of Purim begins with the reading of the story of Esther in the **synagogue**. This continues into the next day.

Children often dress up and perform plays based on the story. Whenever Haman's name is mentioned, children 'boo' loudly or stamp their feet. They may wave a **greggar** (a rattle) to try and stop the name being heard.

The **Talmud** says people should give presents at Purim. People often give two items of food to friends. Some, however, send a book.

Most **Orthodox** Jews believe the events of Purim happened as the book of Esther records them. Many **Reform** Jews are less sure, as there is no other historical record of this story. However, both agree that this story shows how God saves those who trust in Him.

Haman's pockets

In some Jewish areas, the children go from house to house on the festival of Purim, delivering baskets of food. They contain sweet pastries called Hamantaschen, or Haman's pockets.

Haman's pockets are made from circles of pastry, containing poppy seeds. They may be filled with prune or apricot jam, dates, orange, apple, raisins or cream cheese. The circles are folded to form triangles and then baked until they are golden brown.

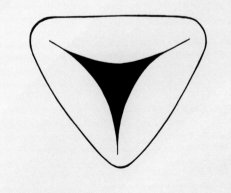

The Western Wall

In this section you will:
- learn about the Western Wall and why it is important to Jews
- think about the importance of places to peoples' religious faith.

The journey of life

Life is like a journey. But does this journey of life have a reason? Or is it just the fun of travelling that matters?

For religious people, making a journey to visit a place that is important to their faith helps them to focus on this faith.

Tale of a temple

When the ancestors of the Jews first began to worship God, they would gather rocks together to mark the place. By the time of Moses, they worshipped in a large tent called the Tabernacle.

Within the Tabernacle was a special area called the Holy of Holies. Inside, there was a box called the **Ark of the Covenant**.

According to the **Tenakh**, this contained two tablets of stone. These were the stones bearing the Ten Commandments that God gave to Moses.

The Tenakh says that King David made Jerusalem his capital city. His son, Solomon, built a temple there.

The temple became the centre for Jewish religion. This was because the Ark of the Covenant, within the Holy of Holies, was so sacred that only the High Priest could visit it on one day in the year.

Secondly, animals were sacrificed in the temple as a way of saying sorry to God for the bad things the people had done, or saying thank you for the good things that God had done for the people.

Invaders destroyed the temple of Solomon. Then it was re-built. Later, invaders also destroyed the second temple.

At the beginning of the first century CE, King Herod had just built a new temple.

In 66 CE, the Jews rebelled against the Romans, who ruled the land at that time. In 70 CE, the Romans set fire to Jerusalem and destroyed the temple, apart from the Western Wall.

The Western Wall today

The Western Wall still stands in the centre of Jerusalem. For many Jews it is a symbol of their hope that one day a new temple will be built there. Many Jews go there to pray.

Today, the Wall is like an open-air synagogue. Men and women stand separately, as they do in an **Orthodox synagogue**. Men wear **kippot** to cover their heads while they pray. Some parents may hold a son's **Bar Mitzvah** there.

Some people write a prayer on paper and place it in a gap in the wall. These pieces of paper have to be removed from time to time.

When the State of Israel was founded in 1948, the Western Wall was in the part of Jerusalem that belonged to the Arab country of Jordan. Above the wall on a hill are the Muslim holy places of the Dome of the Rock and the Black Mosque. In 1967, there was a war and Israel captured the area round the Western Wall. This made it easier for Jews to visit this important site.

Moshe Dayan

Moshe Dayan was a general who led the Israeli army which captured the Western Wall in 1967. He was born on 20 May 1915. Before the capture, he wrote a prayer on a piece of paper and put it in one of the cracks in the wall. His message was one word: '**Shalom**'. This is Hebrew for 'Peace'. Moshe Dayan was praying that the Western Wall, and Israel itself, would know peace.

Later, Moshe Dayan became a politician. He tried to bring all sides in Israel together. However, arguments about the Western Wall and the Temple Mount continue to divide Jews and Arabs to this day. Both sides want control of the area. Moshe Dayan died in 1981.

Masada

Dying for what you believe in?

There are many examples in history where people have preferred to die rather than give up their religion.

Masada made an impressive fortress

Masada today

Masada is a hill, about 150 metres high, that rises out of the desert near the Dead Sea in Israel. It is very hot there – often over 40˚ centigrade. People usually ride up to the top on a cable-car, rather than try to walk up the rocky path.

Archaeologists uncovered the site of Masada in the 1960s. Since then many travellers have visited it. Soldiers in the Israeli army have to run from the bottom of the hill to the top in full kit. Then they promise, 'Masada will not fall again!'

Why Masada became important

In 4 BCE, King Herod the Great built his palace on top of Masada. After his death, the Romans took control of it for a time.

In 66 CE, a Jewish group called the **Zealots** started a civil war against the Romans. One part of this group captured Masada and made it their base. Several families lived there.

In 72 CE, the Romans decided to deal with the Zealots. On Masada the Zealots grew food and had a water supply, and stores of food that would last many years. How could the Romans get the Jews off this hill?

They set up camp round the base of Masada. They put up fences so that no-one could get in or out. They brought an army of slaves to build a ramp up to the fort at the top of the hill. After many months, the Romans reached the top.

The Romans stormed Masada

The leader of the Zealots, Eleazar, told them it was better to die as free people than to be slaves of the Romans. They chose ten men to kill the nine hundred and sixty people who lived there. They set the fortress alight. Then they killed themselves.

When the Romans broke through the walls, they found their enemies dead. Not all the inhabitants died. Two women and five children hid in order to avoid being killed. According to the historian, Josephus, they told the Romans the story of what had happened.

The Romans were impressed by the actions of the Zealots. They also believed it was better to die than to suffer dishonour.

It seemed that in a way it was the Zealots who had won the battle of Masada.

The battle for Masada was just one small conflict in a terrible time for the Jews. Thousands died or lost their homes. Many were taken as slaves to Rome, and had to fight as gladiators in the arena.

Skeletons of Masada

The Israeli archaeologist, Professor Yigael Yadin, found 25 skeletons in a row of caves at Masada in 1963–65. Fourteen of the skeletons were of men, six were of women, four were of children, and there was one tiny baby. They were surrounded by cooking pots and jugs, and the remains of mats, clothes and food.

The Israeli government gave some of the skeletons a state burial. They thought that they were the bodies of Zealots who had died there. They wanted to show that they were proud of these freedom fighters.

However, some of the skeletons were buried with pig bones. The Jews of Masada kept the kosher food laws strictly. It was unlikely that these were Zealots, and they may have been Roman soldiers. That is – unless the Romans buried these bodies with the bones of unclean animals on purpose!

Circumcision – sign of the covenant

In this section you will:
- learn about **circumcision** and why it is important to many Jews today.

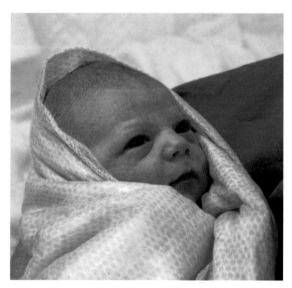

A new life

Stages of life

All through your life there have been special moments. When you were born the people who love you may have had a party. When you left primary school there may have been a final assembly.

Religious people have special ways of celebrating the important moments in life. They have naming ceremonies for new babies. There are 'coming of age' celebrations, and weddings. These special celebrations are called **rites of passage**.

The covenant promise

The birth of a new baby boy or girl is a very happy moment for a Jewish family. Boys have a special ceremony to welcome them into the Jewish community. This is called circumcision.

Circumcision is the removing of the foreskin from a boy's penis. People practised this in ancient times, before Judaism was a faith. Members of some other religions carry it out today. For Jews it is a sign of their **covenant** with God.

Jewish people call the ceremony **Brit Milah**, the 'covenant of circumcision'. It links to the first circumcision that Abraham performed as a sign of this covenant. Here is one of the prayers used at the ceremony:

'Praised be thou, O Lord our God, ruling Spirit of the Universe, who has commanded us to enter into the Covenant of our father Abraham.'

Jewish Prayer Book

Circumcision takes place on the eighth day after the mother has given birth. It can take place in the **synagogue** or in the home of the baby's family. At the synagogue, it happens after morning prayers.

The man who performs the circumcision is called the **mohel**. He is specially trained to do this.

Many Jews believe the spirit of the prophet Elijah is present at every circumcision. There is a special chair – Elijah's Chair. The mohel puts the baby on the chair for a moment, then he gives the baby to the **sandek**.

A party to celebrate a new birth

The sandek is usually one of the baby's grandfathers. He holds the baby on his lap while the operation takes place.

The father recites a special blessing for his son, and the mohel announces the baby's Hebrew name. Most babies have an English name as well.

The whole group now prays that the newly circumcised boy will faithfully follow the **Torah** and be a good person. There is wine for all to drink, and a party to celebrate the life of a new child.

The family takes the foreskin away and buries it as a mark of respect.

Nearly all Jewish boys are circumcised. When the **Reform** Movement began, they asked whether they should continue this practice. However, most decided it was too important to be left out of Jewish rites of passage.

There is also a special naming ceremony for girls. This takes place when they are thirty days old.

Ceremonies for baby boys

Many Jews hold a party on the Friday evening following the birth of a new son. This is an opportunity to celebrate the baby's birth, and to ask God to bless the child with peace throughout his life. They may eat special food, such as lentils, chickpeas, nuts and wine.

On the night before the baby's circumcision, some Jews hold a 'night of watching'. They study special portions of the Torah. They invite children to visit and to sit near the baby boy to recite important prayers, such as the Shema. The adults give the children sweets for helping with this part of the celebration.

Becoming an adult

In this section you will:

● learn about **Bar Mitzvah** and **Bat Mitzvah** ceremonies, and their importance to Jewish people

● think about becoming an adult.

When are you a grown-up?

The French writer Victor Hugo wrote about two people that 'one got older, the other matured'.

When is a person an adult? Is this different from being mature?

British law sets different ages for being mature. You can be held responsible for a crime at ten, drive a car at seventeen, and are allowed to vote at eighteen.

Who matures more quickly? Boys or girls? Most people will regard you as adult when you are responsible.

For Jews, when boys and girls become adult, and full members of their religion they are called Bar Mitzvah or Bat Mitzvah.

Bar Mitzvah

Bar Mitzvah means 'Son of the Commandment'. It is the point at which a boy becomes an adult member of the Jewish community.

He will wear a **tallit** and learn to put on the **tefillin**.

Being Bar Mitzvah does not depend on having a ceremony, but most boys do. This takes place on the **Shabbat** after the boy's thirteenth birthday. He has to learn Hebrew and practise reading the portion of the **Torah** that he has to read in the service. A **rabbi** helps him to do this.

His father says a blessing as he steps up to read.

After the reading, there is usually a special meal to celebrate his Bar Mitzvah. He may make a little speech, thanking his parents and promising to keep the faith.

He is now a full member of the **synagogue**. He can be part of the **minyan**. He is now old enough to keep the fast on **Yom Kippur**.

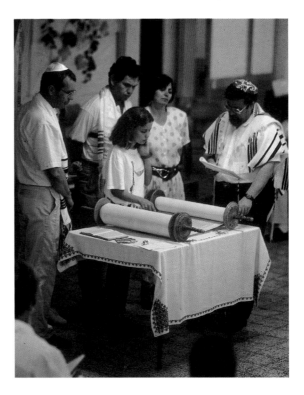

Bat Mitzvah

Reform Jews decided that girls should also have a ceremony to mark their adulthood. This is Bat Mitzvah, which means 'Daughter of the Commandment'. It happens when a girl is twelve. She learns about keeping Shabbat and festivals. She may also read from the Torah.

Orthodox Jews may have a ceremony called **Bat Chayil**, 'Daughter of Worth'. This may take place on a Sunday, rather than Shabbat. She will not read from the Torah, but may read from another part of the **Tenakh**.

Never too old...

Although a Bar Mitzvah normally takes place when a Jewish boy is 13 years old, it is never too late for a man to become Bar Mitzvah.

George Posener was 88 years old when he became Bar Mitzvah. His parents were not religious, so he had not had a Bar Mitzvah as a teenager. As he grew older, he decided to have the ceremony. He was one of six adults who became Bar Mitzvah at the Beth El-Keser synagogue in New Haven, USA.

Another older person who became Bar Mitzvah was a 71-year-old man who learned to read Hebrew when he joined his local synagogue at the age of 67!

Getting married

Why get married?

What sort of person would you like to marry?

Many people today decide to live together without being married. However, people do still have a marriage ceremony. Why?

Religious people may want to make their promises in front of God and their religious community. Others may want to state publicly their love for each other.

Marriage is about commitment

The Jewish wedding ceremony

Most Jewish families are happy if their children marry other Jews. This is because they will bring up their children in the faith and there is no conflict. A child born of a Jewish mother is Jewish. If a Jewish man 'marries out' this can cause problems within the family.

Some Jews might encourage the non-Jewish partner to convert to Judaism. They may ask them to promise they will bring up their children in the Jewish faith.

In Hebrew, marriage is called **kiddushin**, which means 'holy', as Jews believe marriage is holy.

Before the wedding, the bridegroom signs a marriage contract, the **Ketubah**. In it, he promises to take care of his wife.

The marriage can take place on any day except **Shabbat**, and may be held in the **synagogue**. The bride, groom and witnesses stand under a **huppah**, a canopy on four poles.

The **rabbi** conducts the ceremony, but a **cantor** may sing the blessings. The first blessing welcomes the bride and groom:

'Blessed is the one who comes in the name of the Lord.'

The huppah stands for the new home the couple will make together.

The bride and groom take a sip of wine from the same glass. The groom then places a ring on the right hand forefinger of his bride and says a blessing. He may read out the promises he has made in the Ketubah. The cantor will then sing seven blessings for the couple.

The bridegroom then takes the wine glass and wraps it in cloth. He places it on the floor and stamps on it. This is a symbolic act. It says that marriage will have to face bad times as well as good. It also reminds them that the temple in Jerusalem was destroyed and has never been re-built.

After the formal ceremony, there is a wedding reception. Since no marriages are allowed on Shabbat, Sundays and Tuesdays are the most popular days for this ceremony.

Marriage

Are marriages made in heaven? Many Jews believe that when two people fall in love and get married, God has already chosen them as partners in marriage.

The **Talmud** teaches that 40 days before a person is conceived, God has already decided which two people should be married. The Talmud also says that a 'good match' is a miracle. It is as great as that of the escape of the people of Israel from Egypt. One scholar, called Maimonides, said that God rewards or even punishes people by the partner He chooses for them to marry!

Many Jewish people consult a 'matchmaker' to help them find the right partner. In recent years, some Jews have turned to Internet matchmaking websites.

The bridal party meet under the huppah

Death

In this section you will:
- learn about Jewish ideas concerning death and mourning
- think about your own ideas about what happens when we die.

Ultimate statistic

The writer George Bernard Shaw said that death is the ultimate statistic: every one of us dies!

We all have to face the fact that we will die. How does religion help people face death? Does religion help us to think about the really important question: is this life all there is?

Jewish funerals

A truly observant Jew, if they know they are about to die, tries to recite the **Shema** and to ask God to forgive their sins.

Orthodox Jews insist that their dead must be buried, though **Reform** Jews may allow cremation. The funeral takes place, if possible, within twenty-four hours of the death.

As soon as the family hears of the death of a loved one, they make small tears in their clothes, as a sign of their grief.

A close relative prepares the body for burial. They wash the body and wrap it in a plain linen shroud (burial cloth). Men may be wrapped in their **tallit**.

A Jewish graveyard

As the body is lowered into the ground, the **rabbi** recites the **kaddish**, a special prayer for mourning and remembrance.

May God's great name be blessed, forever and ever.

May God's name be blessed, praised, glorified, revered, held in awe, acclaimed and revered – though it is higher than all the blessings, songs, praises and consolations that can be spoken in this world.

May Heaven grant a universal peace and life for us and for all Israel, Amen.

Extract from the kaddish

Mourning

Judaism encourages people who have lost a loved one to grieve.

For the first week, the family sits **shiva**. The word means 'seven'. The close family members stay at home and others visit them. They offer comfort, and pray with the family. Traditionally, the mourners sit on low chairs during this week. This symbolizes that the whole body is 'brought low' by grief. Male mourners recite kaddish.

For the month after the funeral, there is **sheloshin**, which means 'thirty'. Male mourners visit the **synagogue** every day to recite kaddish. After this, things begin to return to normal, although observant Jews will not go to parties for a year after the death of a close relative, out of respect.

The third stage is **Yahrzeit** ('year-time'). On the first anniversary of the death, a Jewish family lights a candle. This remembers the verse from Proverbs,

'A person's soul is the candle of the Lord.' They give thanks to God for the life of the one who has died. Close family members will hold Yahrzeit every year on the anniversary of the death of their loved one.

Jews may have a gravestone with the person's name engraved on it. It is a tradition to place small stones on the grave at each visit. Abraham marked Sarah's grave like this.

Jews believe that God will reward a person who has led a good life. God will also judge the wicked. Jews believe that the 'after life' is in the hands of God, and not something to think about now.

Thinking about death

Jews believe that death is as natural as life. It is part of God's plan for all people. Here are some thoughts by Jews on the topic of dying.

'I don't mind dying. I just don't want to be there when it happens.'

Woody Allen

'Dust you are and to dust you will return.'

Genesis 3: 19

'Poets and philosophers sometimes have a go at praising death… But we observe that, like the rest of us, they usually work hard at staying alive.'

Hermann Wouk

God's world or ours?

In this section you will:

- learn more about Jewish beliefs about the environment and the need to care for the planet
- learn about Jewish teaching about pets.

Tu B'Shvat

Tu B'Shvat is the festival of tree planting – a 'New Year for Trees'. It comes at the end of the harvest. In Israel, people try to plant new trees as a sign that they are willing to give back to the land as well as to take from it.

The Torah on animals

Jews believe that the seven laws given to Noah, The **Noachide Laws**, apply to all people (see page 50). The fourth of these laws is 'Be kind to animals'.

The **Torah** also encourages Jewish people to help animals:

'If you see your friend's ass or his ox has fallen on the road, you must help him raise it.'

Deuteronomy 22: 4

A balance of nature

A **rabbi** once said 'The world follows its own habit'. This means that God intended that there should be balances in nature.

Jews believe that it is their responsibility to keep this balance.

Planting trees is a sign of hope and thankfulness

Noah's Ark

God is the creator. Human beings are his stewards. It is their task to look after things and not spoil the world for future generations.

The rowing boat

Some people use the story of Noah as a story with a meaning. It means that if you want to be obedient to God, one way is to show that you care for the environment. This is what Noah did when he obeyed God's call to rescue the animals.

A group of Jewish teachers said people should think about the environment in this way: we have a responsibility to life. We must protect it. This world is like a great ark (boat) and we are all passengers in it. This world is fragile, and we must work together to protect it.

Jewish teaching on pets

For Jews, looking after animals is an important responsibility. Jewish rules about animals say that pet owners must feed their pets before they feed themselves. They may walk their dog on **Shabbat** because most Jews do not see this as work. Most Jews allow their pets to eat non-**kosher** food – as long as the Jewish owner does not eat it, too!

Jews should never be cruel to animals. De-clawing cats and docking the ears or tails of dogs is not allowed.

Creation and the environment

In this section you will:
- learn about the Jewish idea of creation
- read about the Jewish understanding of God as a shepherd who cares for the earth.

What a wonderful world

Have you ever seen something of such beauty that you felt deep emotion? Or had a personal experience that has really moved you? Everyone can experience a sense of wonder – not just religious people.

Religious people may find these experiences make them think about what matters most. Jewish people may reflect on the idea of God as a creator.

The Noachide Laws

Jews believe that everyone, Jewish or not, should follow the laws that God gave to Noah after the flood.

1. Do not worship **idols**.
2. Do not murder.
3. Do not steal.
4. Avoid sexual misconduct.
5. Be kind to animals.
6. Avoid blasphemy.
7. Worship only one God.

Creation

The **Torah** teaches that God is the creator, and that all that exists comes from God.

The story of creation in Genesis says that God created the world in six days, and rested on the seventh day. Some people believe that this is literally true. Others believe the story is not about *how* God created the world, but *why*.

At the end of each day of creation, the Torah says, 'God saw that it was very good.' Jewish people believe that God gave human beings a special trust to care for the planet. Humans are responsible if things go wrong.

'God blessed them [man and woman] and said "Be fruitful and increase; fill the earth and subdue it; have dominion over the fish in the sea, the birds of the air and every living thing that moves on the earth."'

Genesis 1: 28

| Day 1 | Day 2 | Day 3 | Day 4 | Day 5 | Day 6 | Day 7 |

The Genesis creation calendar

'The heavens show the glory of God, the sky makes known his handiwork.'

Psalm 19: 1

In the past, many Jews thought this meant that human beings could use the environment how they saw fit. Now, most Jews would say that humans must work with God to care for the world about them.

There are ideas in the Torah about caring for and improving the world. For example, **Shabbat** is a rest for animals as well as people. The earth must 'rest' for a year after every seven years, so that it is refreshed.

Even armies must take care:

'When in your war against a city you have to besiege it for a long time in order to capture it, you must not destroy its trees…You may eat (the fruit) of them, but you must not cut them down.'

Deuteronomy 20: 19

The Lord is my Shepherd

Jacob, Moses and David were all shepherds. Their job meant that they cared for animals. The best-known of David's songs, Psalm 23, begins:

'The Lord is my shepherd; I shall not want.
He makes me lie down in green pastures;
he leads me beside still waters,
he restores my soul.'

(New Revised Standard Version)

The Torah teaches that humans may eat animals for food, wear their skins, and use the parts of animals for any good purpose. The Torah is written on parchment. Parchment is made from the skin of goats or sheep.

Moral issues

In this section you will:
- learn about Jewish beliefs concerning money, family and drugs
- read some Jewish thoughts about family issues.

Morality

Morality has to do with choosing between right and wrong. Some people think that their conscience tells them what to do. Others, especially religious people, think that you can find out what God wants you to do by turning to the scriptures.

Money

Many Jews have a small collection box in their homes called **pushkes**. They give money regularly to charities such as Jewish Care, which looks after the elderly and disabled.

The Ten Commandments warn people not to steal, or even to want things that are not theirs. There are many teachings about wealth:

'Be wise enough not to wear yourself out trying to get rich.'

Proverbs 23: 7

'Since there will never cease to be some in need on the earth, I therefore command you, "Open your hand to the poor and needy neighbour in your land."'

Deuteronomy 15: 11

The **Talmud** (see page 31) tells how being poor is a miserable state, and people should help others to escape poverty.

Family life

'Honour your father and your mother so that your days may be long in the land that the Lord is giving you.'

Exodus 20: 12

Jews believe that a family is an important part of society. This is where people learn to love one another and where children receive their first education. Jews believe children should care for their parents when they become older.

Jews also see the family as an important place where the religion is passed on.

Family life is important to Jewish people

This is where children learn about the important festivals, the food laws, and other aspects of what it means to be Jewish.

Parents are responsible for bringing up their children properly. The Talmud advises: 'Teach your son a trade or you teach him to become a robber.'

Marriage is important to Jews. It is within marriage that two people develop and become fully mature. Only in rare cases does a divorce take place.

Alcohol

Jews are allowed to drink alcohol. They use wine in religious ceremonies. However, they do not approve of heavy drinking. The **Midrash** says, 'Wine enters, sense goes out; wine enters, secrets come out.'

Jewish judges are not allowed to pass judgement if they have drunk even one glass of wine. They must wait until the alcohol has passed from their body.

Drugs

Jews believe that drugs should only be used for medical reasons. Many Jews campaign against the misuse of drugs.

They believe that human beings are made 'in the image of God'. Hence they must care for their bodies in a responsible way.

Drugs can bring all kinds of problems

Family issues

The Jewish writer Rebbetzin Feige Twerski offers advice to Jewish parents on an Internet website (http://www.aish.com). Here are some of his tips found on how to bring up children.

Respect your child as a person. King Solomon said, 'Raise each child according to his or her individual path.'

Offer love at the same time as any criticism. Say, 'This behaviour is not like you.' This shows the high opinion that the father has of the child.

For every criticism, give five words of praise.

Remember that happy parents make for happy children!

Finally – pray, pray and pray some more!

Why is there suffering?

In this section you will:
- learn how Jewish people have suffered anti-Semitism
- think about **scapegoating** and how this is part of anti-Semitism.

Scapegoating

Sometimes particular people are picked on or bullied, when others are left alone. Maybe it is because of the colour of their hair, or because they wear glasses, or speak differently or have a different colour skin.

Sometimes one group of people picks on another, smaller group and blames them for everything that is bad in their own lives. This can be called scapegoating.

It is named after a practice the ancestors of the Jews used to do when they lived in deserts. A priest would choose a goat, and recite over the goat's head all the sins of the people. They drove the goat out into the desert to take away the sins from the people.

People today use scapegoats to take away their anger or sense of failure.

Jewish suffering before the Holocaust

In 70 CE, the Romans destroyed the temple in Jerusalem. They forced Jews to leave Israel. The Jews went to live in countries in North Africa and Europe. This event is known as the **diaspora**, which means 'scattering'.

When the Roman Empire became Christian, this led to problems for many Jews.

People were prejudiced against Jews. Christians often thought this was justified, because, they said, Jews had allowed Jesus to be crucified. Jesus was Jewish, but those who hated Jews ignored this important fact.

In 1066 CE, there were Jews in England. The Christian church did not allow its members to be money-lenders. They forced Jews to do this.

In 1290 CE, King Edward expelled Jews from England. They were not allowed to return until the seventeenth century.

In Europe, many people attacked Jews. In Russia the Tsars (rulers in Russia) encouraged the army to attack Jews. Over a million Jews left Russia in the 1880s CE. Non-Jewish Russians helped the Tsar's army to persecute Jews. They drove them away from their homes and destroyed their houses and their possessions.

Over 100,000 Russian and Polish Jews came to England and others went to the USA. They set up new businesses and schools.

The scandal of Captain Dreyfus

In the 1890s CE, Captain Dreyfus, an army officer, was falsely accused of spying for Germany.

In the early twentieth century, many Jews began to move to the country of Palestine. They set up **kibbutzim** (communal farms) and built the city of Tel Aviv on land they bought from the local Arab people.

Captain Alfred Dreyfus

Dreyfus was Jewish. Many people thought that this was the reason why he was accused – not because there was any evidence against him.

Dreyfus was given a life sentence. However, many famous people campaigned and Dreyfus was eventually released.

A young Swiss journalist, Theodor Hertzl, wrote about the case. He said that as long as Jews lived in Europe, they would always be victims. They needed a country of their own. This would be the new Israel. The idea is called **Zionism**.

Simon Wiesenthal

In 1945, the Second World War ended, and the prisoners were set free from the **concentration camps**. Some Jews felt that the people who committed the crimes of the **Holocaust** should be brought to trial. The most famous of these was Simon Wiesenthal, a Jew who had survived the concentration camps himself. He helped to capture Adolf Eichmann in 1960. Eichmann was a Nazi who fled from Europe to South America.

The Simon Wiesenthal Centre was set up in Los Angeles, USA, in 1997. It has offices in several countries, and more than 400,000 members. The centre still works to bring the guilty to trial. It runs a website where people can log on to find out and share information about suspected war criminals. It also runs educational courses so that people can learn about the Holocaust.

The Holocaust

In this section you will:
- learn about the **Holocaust** and Jewish suffering at this time
- read about Yad Vashem, a museum dedicated to Jews who died in the Holocaust.

The Holocaust

'Holocaust' means 'burnt offering'. The word refers to the suffering of the Jews from 1933–45 in Europe. Adolf Hitler, leader of the Nazi Party in Germany, began by banning Jews from parks, theatres and universities. His Nazi Party organized book-burnings and attacks against Jewish businesses. At the start of World War II the Nazis set up **concentration camps**. They intended to kill all Jews in Europe.

Escape from Sobibor

There were many concentration camps from which people had little hope of escaping. However, on 14 October 1943, over 300 Jews escaped from the camp of Sobibor. A quarter of a million Jews had been murdered there. Every day, trains arrived carrying thousands of people from Nazi-occupied Europe. As they got off the trains, they were divided into two groups.

Those who could work were taken to one side. Those who could not – older people, women with children – were taken to gas chambers and killed. It took about fifteen to twenty minutes to die.

A group of prisoners stole some weapons and killed their guards. Their leaders encouraged them to escape.

Over 600 prisoners rushed the gates and took on the other guards. Many were shot, and others died when they stepped on land-mines outside the camp. But about 300 managed to escape.

Some religious Jews refused to go, as they knew they would have to break the commandment 'You shall not kill'. For all that the Nazis had done to them, they did not believe it was right to fight back.

After the escape, the Nazis closed the camp and buried it. Now, in the woods around Sobibor, there is a statue in memory of those who died there. It has the words 'Never Again' carved in the stone.

The concentration camps were so awful that many Jews stopped believing in a God of love. Others became religious, as they came to believe that there had to be One who was better than human beings.

The Chief **Rabbi**, Dr Jonathan Sacks, wrote:

'We will never understand the Holocaust. But the asking of questions is itself a religious act. Future generations will ask: Why do we keep on being Jews? The answer is: To tell the story of our death sentence and our survival. And if they do not ask, we must make them ask.'

God is hanging

Ellie Wiesel wrote a book about his time in a concentration camp. It is called *Night*. He tells this story:

'The SS hanged two Jewish men and a youth in front of the whole camp. The men died quickly, but the death throes of the youth lasted for half an hour.

'"Where is God? Where is he?" someone asked behind me.

'As the youth hung in torment in the noose after a long time, I heard a man call again, "Where is God now?"

'And I heard a voice in myself, "Where is he? He is hanging there on the gallows."'

Yad Vashem

Yad Vashem means 'The hand of the name', meaning 'The hand of God'. It is the name of a museum in Jerusalem on the theme of the suffering of the Jewish people during the Holocaust.

At Yad Vashem, there are paintings by hundreds of children who died in the concentration camps. The Nazis murdered more than one and a half million children between 1939 and 1945. There is also a room which has the names of the main concentration camps written on its floor. There is a flame which burns constantly as a reminder of the people who died.

Many Jewish families have brought tombstones of their murdered relatives, and placed them at Yad Vashem.

In this section you will:

● learn more about Jewish ideas about God

● learn how that affects the way they live.

Job's faith was tested by God

Does God exist?

'The fool says in his heart, "There is no God. Everyone is evil, every deed is bad, No one does any good!"'

Psalm 14: 1

Jews usually say that to be Jewish, you must believe in God. However, there are some Jews who follow some of the religious laws and festivals who do not believe in God.

The question for most Jews is not 'does God exist?', but 'what sort of being is God?'

A famous story tells how, in one of the **concentration camps**, some Jews put God on trial for ignoring their pain. They decided this God did not care. They found God 'guilty' of letting his people down. After the trial, they went off to worship the God they found guilty.

In the story in the **Tenakh**, Job has to learn that God alone is in control. He says,

'The Lord gives and the Lord takes away; Blessed be the name of the Lord.'

Job 1: 21

Jews believe that God cannot be proved or disproved by argument. God has to be experienced.

What is God like?

Jews believe that God has always been there. God has no beginning and no end: God has always existed.

Jews believe that God created everything that exists out of nothing. God continues to create things. Human beings help in this work.

The **Shema** teaches that God is one. Jews believe that God is holy and God is good.

God is in control.

God cannot be represented by an image or an **idol**. The name of God is too holy to be known. Many Jewish books do not print the name of God. Even the word 'God' is represented 'G-D'.

Jews must only worship this one true God.

God is Spirit and is eternal. God knows everything that has happened and that will happen.

God is the Lord of History and makes things better. By giving the law through Moses and sending his messengers, the **prophets**, God shows that he cares for the world and the chosen people.

God is the one true judge. He punishes evil and rewards those who live as He wants them to live.

The universe: creation or accident?

Who is God?

It is very hard to describe what God is like. The following words are some of the ways in which Jews try to describe God. They paint a picture of a God who is always present, and who loves all people.

'In the beginning, God was…'

Genesis 1: 1

'Who among the gods is like you, O Lord? Who is like you – majestic in holiness, awesome in glory, working wonders?'

Exodus 15: 11

'I waited patiently for the Lord; he turned to me and heard my cry.
He lifted me out of the slimy pit, out of the mud and mire;
He set my feet upon a rock and gave me a firm place to stand.'

Psalm 40: 1–2

'In every place where you find the imprint of men's feet – there am I.'

The Talmud

Glossary

Agadah stories in the Talmud to help people

Agnostic someone who is not sure whether there is a God

Amidah a prayer with eighteen blessings to God

Aron Hakodesh/Ark of the Covenant the cupboard where the Torah and other scrolls are stored in the synagogue

Ashkenazim Jews whose ancestors came from Central and Eastern Europe

Atheist a person who believes there is no God

Atonement being at one with God

Bar Mitzvah 'Son of the Commandment'; a boy who reaches Jewish adulthood at age thirteen

Bat Chayil 'Daughter of Excellence'; a ceremony for girls reaching the age of twelve

Bat Mitzvah 'Daughter of the Commandment'; a girl who reaches Jewish adulthood at the age of twelve

Bet Din 'House of Justice'; a Jewish court of law

Bet ha Knesset 'House of Assembly'; Hebrew name for a synagogue

Bimah raised platform in a synagogue where the Torah is read

Brit milah covenant of circumcision

Challah (plural **-ot**) special plaited loaves of bread for Shabbat and festivals

Cantor the person who leads prayers in the synagogue

Cheder religion classes for Jewish children

Circumcision removal of the foreskin from the penis for religious or health reasons

Concentration camps camps organized by the Nazis in World War II for the murder of Jews and other groups they disapproved of

Covenant the promise made by God to care for the Jewish people

Diaspora 'dispersion'; the name given to Jews living outside Israel

Exodus (1) the escape from Egypt led by Moses; (2) second book of the Torah

Fast to go without food for a religious reason

Genocide mass destruction of a whole race of people

Greggar wooden rattle used whenever Haman's name is spoken in the telling of the story of Esther

Halakhah the laws of Judaism

Hanukiah eight-branched candlestick used at Hanukkah

Hanukkah an eight-day festival of lights

Havdalah 'separation'; the ceremony marking the end of Shabbat

Holocaust the murder of over six million Jews by Nazis in Europe 1933–45. Also known as Shoah

Huppah the canopy under which a Jewish couple are married

Idol a statue worshipped as a god

Judaism the religion of Jewish people

Kaddish a prayer of praise to God said by a mourner

Ketubah the marriage contract

Ketuvim 'writings'; the third section of the Tenakh

Kibbutz a communal farm or settlement

Kiddush prayer of blessing said at the beginning of Shabbat

Kiddushin 'sanctification'; a Jewish marriage

Kippah (plural**–ot**) head covering worn by Jews

Knesset Israeli Parliament

Kosher food that Jews are allowed to eat

Magen David Adom 'Shield of David'; a six-pointed star emblem

Manna bread provided for the Israelites when they escaped from Egypt

Menorah six-branched candlestick

Messiah 'the anointed one of God'; a king-like figure who God will send at the end of time

Mezuzah a miniature scroll in a case, fixed to the right door-post of Jewish homes

Midrash a collection of commentaries on the Tenakh

Mikveh pool for Jewish ritual bathing

Minyan minimum number of adults needed for public worship, usually ten

Miracle an act of God that suspends the laws of nature

Mishnah Jewish religious books, collection of teachings of the rabbis

Mitzvot 'commandments'; Jewish religious laws; good deeds

Mohel person who performs circumcisions

Monotheism belief in the existence of only one God

Ner Tamid the eternal light kept burning in a synagogue

Nevi'im the writings of the prophets and historical books in the Tenakh

Noachide Laws the seven laws given to Noah that Jews regard as basic rules for morality for all human beings

Oral law teachings based on the laws in the Torah, later written down in the Mishnah and the Talmud

Orthodox Jews Jews who observe traditional Jewish teachings and uphold Orthodoxy

Patriarch founding father of a religion

Pesach Hebrew for Passover; festival to remind Jews how God rescued them from slavery in Egypt

Prophet messenger of God

Purim festival to remember how Esther rescued the Jews from death

Pushkes charity collection box in a Jewish home

Rabbi spiritual leader and teacher in a Jewish community

Reform Jews Jews who felt that Judaism had to change to fit in with modern society

Repent be sorry and try to change the way you live

Rites of passage special ceremonies that mark an important event in life such as birth or marriage

Rosh Hashanah Jewish New Year

Sandek the person who holds a baby boy at his circumcision

Scapegoat the person who is blamed for the misfortunes of a group

Sephardim Jews whose ancestors came from Mediterranean countries such as Spain, North Africa and the Middle East

Shabbat Jewish holy day, also known as Sabbath

Shalom Hebrew for 'peace'

Sheloshim thirty days of mourning after the death of a relative

Shema 'Hear!'; the Jewish prayer stating the oneness of God

Shiva 'seven'; the first seven days after the death of a relative

Shoah 'destruction'; another name for the Holocaust

Shofar ram's horn used during synagogue services and festivals

Siddur Jewish prayer-book

Sidra portion of the Torah read during synagogue services

Synagogue Jewish place of worship

Tallit prayer robe or shawl worn by Jews during morning prayer

Talmud collection of writings about Jewish laws and teachings

Tefillin two leather boxes containing biblical verses, worn for morning prayer on weekdays

Tenakh Hebrew name for the Bible. It contains the Torah, Nevi'im and Ketuvim

Theist a person who believes in the existence of a god

Torah 'instruction'; name given to the first five books of the Tenakh, or sometimes to the whole Bible, and sometimes to all rabbinic literature

Vocation a calling by God for a special task or purpose

Warden person in charge of organizing synagogue services

Yad pointer used when reading from the Torah scrolls

Yarhzeit Yiddish for annual remembrance of the death of a loved one

Yeshiva college for rabbis and students of Jewish scripture and traditions

Yom Kippur Day of Atonement

Zealots Jewish freedom fighters from the first century CE

Zionism belief in the need for a Jewish homeland based in the Middle East with Jerusalem as its capital

Index